WILLIAM *and the* EX-PRIME MINISTER

Carol Ann Duffy

ANVIL PRESS POETRY

William and the Ex-Prime Minister

William said it stood to reason,
though his Outlaws chorused *Garn!*
William didn't think it treason
locking her in the Ole Barn.

She was only Grantham's daughter,
William came of sterner stuff.
Through his veins coursed lic'rice water.
William Brown had had enough.

William stood upon a soapbox,
said *She is a norful sort.*
Half the country reckons hope's lost.
Jolly well resign, she ought.

She can moan an' she can grumble,
what I say is She Mus' Go!
No one likes her, even Jumble
barked at her. Jus' goes to show.

From the barn came threats of thcreaming
(she could thcream till she was thick).
William's freckled face was gleaming
with resolve. He waved his stick.

Outlaws! Pirates! Band of Injuns!
We'll go down in History.
Never mind the Heaths and St Johns,
they'll put statchoos up to me!

William's father, William's brother
grimly marched across the fields . . .
William's teacher . . . William's mother . . .
William (*crumbs!*) took to his heels.

Nemesis caught up with William
as he crawled along the ditch.
But there's thousands jobless! Millions!
Thanks to that narsy ole witch.

Later, William, walking sadly
knew his struggle not in vain
when, meeting him en route to Hadley,
William beat up Hubert Lane.

The Tory Candidate,
On the Eve of the General Election,
Gets Down on His Knees

Look here. That is to say, Almighty God,
the thing is, I haven't a snowball's chance in Hell.
Sorry. Last time round was all very well,
but the voters are sick to death of the iron rod.

I blame the Unemployed. The idle sods
won't do a thing to help themselves. A spell
of National Service is the answer, I can tell.
Short shocks, smart uniforms and healthy bods.

Entre nous, if you could pull a few strings,
I'll put the money up to mend the Church roof.
Play the game, I'm not asking for bloody wings.

Quiet sort of cove, aren't you? To tell the truth,
I think you're a bit of a pinko. Little things
give you away. Those loaves and fishes . . . 'Struth!

The Bore's Prayer

At the end of the day, all things taken
into account, it's only fair to say
what God has given he can take away,
unless I am very much mistaken.

Unless I am very much mistaken,
each, in his own way, has a part to play.
Amen to that. Where there's a will there's a way.
Somebody's got to bring home the bacon,

so to speak. I've never been one to doubt
these things. What's good enough for the Pope
is good enough for me. You get nowt for nowt

in this life. Give some people enough rope
and we all know what. There's no need to shout
the odds. Touch wood, Yours Truly lives in hope.

The Prayer of the Magician's Assistant

Christ, the things you have to do to earn a buck.
His nerves jangling, my bra spangling, top hats,
wands, rabbits and twelve doves. Now these soft prats
think he can saw me in half. Can he fuck.

Some nights I wish he'd get it wrong, run out of luck
and smash the wrong wrist-watch. *Get out of that,
Sweetie*, I'd smile smugly. If only a fat
man, pissed, would sit on the Mindreading Duck.

So I'm in the box and he's sawing away . . .
Jesus, that drumroll! Any half-baked, dud
magician could do this. The punters pray.

But something is wrong. He sweats. *This is no good,
you fool*, I hiss . . . the last thing he hears me say
as the saw slides out, silver, smeared with blood.

The Professor of Philosophy Attempts Prayer

If a then b, if Me then Thee. If not y
then not x. Why not? I cannot believe
in my own arm when it's under my sleeve,
nor in the Good, no matter how much I try.

I see that feathered things are made to fly
but are they *really there*? What I perceive
to be ain't necessarily so. I'll die
well-off, but with nothing of value to leave.

If not not pigeon, then there is a pigeon,
though I do not accept this as true.
I have enough trouble with birds . . . but religion?

As for the Virgin Birth . . . if p then q
rubbishes that. Lord, give me a smidgen
of proof, and I'll not not not believe in you.

The Dyslexic Philosopher

for Ian Duhig

How to make sense of the world?
Why am I her?
Is the table for real?
Is the choir?

Who to make sense of the world?
What is the thurt?
Is perception kayo
nad si thought?

What is the pinto of life?
Is it to be
to be do be do be
or do tie?

What does it mean, all of this?
Is it a drame?
Can I know all of shit
in a name?

Can I ownk?
Can I nowk?
Can I wonk?

And is there a Dog?

Dear Writer-in-Residence

Dear Writer-in-Residence, I enclose my verse
(94 poems) it's three weeks' work.
I'll call in next week, which is time enough
for you to read, digest and admire the stuff.

Just some background info – despite all my labours
I had a very curt note from a bloke at Fabers.
Chatto & Windus haven't bothered to reply.
(They've had it a *fortnight*.) Who else should I try?

Penguin? Bloodaxe? See what you think.
Needless to say, I'll buy you a drink
when the MS is accepted. THIS IS VITAL.
(What do you reckon to *Thoughts and Other Poems* for the title?)

I don't know your own work – I haven't much time
to read modern poets and I bet it doesn't rhyme.
But I hope, as a professional, you won't plagiarize
any of my best lines. (A word to the wise!!)

The illustrations will arrive under separate cover –
30 watercolours © my wife's old mother.
I'll quite understand if there's not room for them all,
but I insist on the retention of 'Mankind's Fall'.

I look forward to hearing from you within five days –
(just dash off a thousand words of closely reasoned praise.)
I can cope with the fame OK. (Champagne! Venison!!)
Good luck with the residency. Sincerely, Alf Tennyson.

Fuckinelle

The poet's tried to write a villanelle
and modestly declares so on the night.
He's very proud. The audience can tell.

Drunk Dylan Thomas wrote in this way well
and raged against the dying of the light.
The poet's tried to write a villanelle.

In certain magazines this work can sell.
They published it, to *our* writer's delight.
He's very proud, the audience can tell.

He reads it like the tinkling of a bell.
Each syllable must fall exactly right.
The poet's tried to write a villanelle.

To be so talented must be sheer hell.
No matter if his subject matter's trite,
he's very proud, the audience can tell.

As moving as the death of Little Nell,
the reading drones on far into the night.
The poet's tried to write a villanelle,
he's very proud. The audience can see that.

Make That a Large One

I could've been famous, could've been rich,
but Fortune dropped me like a loose stitch.
One for the road. Another for the gutter.
Set 'em up, J-J-Joe.

I stutter, but could've played Hamlet,
could've played Lear, if things had
worked out well that year. Now,
alone in a bar, spirits sinking,

I could've been anything.

Me.

Wishful drinking.

Still Life with Hangover

You notice a strange vase on your dressing-table. *Groan.*
To the left of the vase is a mouth-organ. *Moan.*
You begin to wonder where all those five-pound notes
came from. There is worse. Pale sunlight
strikes that vase. At the end of the bed, a foot
pokes out. Not yours. *Christ.* In the mirror
you have signed your name. Lipstick. Piss artist.

Rounds

Eight pints
of lager, please,
and, of draught Guinness, nine;
two glasses of pale ale – a squeeze
of lemon in that port – a dry white wine,
four rums, three G-and-Ts, a vodka – that's the lot.
On second thoughts, you'd better give me one more double scotch.

A half
of scrumpy here
and, over there, a stout.
I think we're ready for more beer;
ten brandies, three martinis – no, my shout!
A triple advocaat with lemonade and lime
and six Bacardis – make that twelve, I've just noticed the time.

Six calves
of harlsberg – fast –
pine bitter shandies – tents –
and make the landies barge; a vast
treasure of mipple X, ten mème de crenthes,
nine muddy blaries and, of winger gine, a wealth.
Got that? And then the rame again all sound and one yourself.

Write About *Happiness*

What does happiness look like?
You in your red coat.
Where does it go for a drink?
To bed, on Sundays.

What does happiness sound like?
The purr of an unhooked phone.
What does it do for a living?
It has private means.

What does happiness feel like?
The barehanded planting of bulbs.
What is its home address?
Yours, sweetheart.

Does happiness have a scent?
The sea, the air, the earth.
Where did you see it last?
Under the bedclothes, laughing.

What taste does happiness have?
That of a long, slow kiss.
And how does happiness write?
Badly, like this.

For Adrian Henri

ACKNOWLEDGEMENTS

Some of these poems were first published
in *Ambit, Poetry and Audience* and
Thrown Voices (Turret Books, 1986).

Published in 1992
by Anvil Press Poetry Ltd
69 King George Street London SE10 8PX
ISBN 0 85646 253 5 (signed)
      0 85646 254 3 (unsigned)

Copyright © Carol Ann Duffy 1992

This edition is limited to one thousand
numbered copies of which nos. 1–300
are signed by the poet

Anvil Press Poetry acknowledges
the financial assistance
of The Arts Council

Designed and composed by Anvil
Photoset in Plantin by Wordstream
Printed by Morganprint Blackheath Ltd